THE MONEY MAGNET

By

Mr. George k. Williams

Table of content

Chapter 8
Investing in yourself

Chapter 9
Creating multiple income streams

Introduction

"The Money Magnet" is a term used to describe a person or entity that attracts wealth and abundance effortlessly. It refers to a state of being in which an individual's thoughts, beliefs, and actions align with the energy of money and abundance, allowing them to attract financial success and prosperity. This concept is based on the principles of the law of attraction, which suggests that like attracts like, and that our thoughts and emotions shape our reality. The idea behind the money magnet is that by adopting a positive mindset, taking inspired action, and aligning with the energy of abundance, anyone can become a magnet for wealth and success.

Chapter 1
The money mindset

The idea of a "money mindset" alludes to the convictions, mentalities, and propensities that shape our relationship with cash. Our cash outlook is framed by various elements, including our childhood, social foundation, encounters with cash, and individual qualities. Fostering a solid cash outlook can assist us with making monetary strength and progress, while a negative cash mentality can prompt monetary pressure and issues.

A few normal qualities of a positive cash outlook include:

1.   A spotlight on overflow: Individuals with a positive cash outlook accept that there is sufficient cash to go around and that chances to bring in and set aside money are plentiful.

2.   A readiness to face challenges: A positive cash mentality includes an eagerness to proceed with well balanced plans of action to accomplish monetary

objectives, like putting resources into stocks or beginning a business.

3.   A feeling of appreciation: Those with a good cash mentality perceive the worth of what they have and are thankful for the open doors they need to bring in and set aside money.

4.   A obligation to monetary obligation: A positive cash outlook includes getting a sense of ownership with one's monetary circumstance and coming to insightful conclusions about spending and saving.

1.   An receptiveness to learning: Individuals with a positive cash outlook are continuously able to learn new things about overseeing cash and are available to novel thoughts and procedures.

Then again, a negative cash mentality can be portrayed by:

1.   A spotlight on shortage: Individuals with a negative cash mentality accept that there will never be sufficient cash and that

chances to bring in and set aside money are restricted.

2.   A feeling of dread toward facing challenges: A pessimistic cash outlook implies an anxiety toward facing challenges and a conviction that any speculation or monetary choice will definitely prompt disappointment.

3.   A propensity for selfishness: Those with a negative cash mentality might feel qualified for cash and view it as something that ought to be given to them as opposed to something they need to work for.

4.   A absence of monetary obligation: A negative cash mentality includes an absence of obligation regarding what is going on and an inclination to pursue imprudent or untrustworthy monetary choices.

5.   A shut mindedness: Individuals with a negative cash outlook might be impervious to novel thoughts and procedures for overseeing cash, it is only one "right" method for getting things done to trust that there.

It's critical to take note of that our cash attitude isn't firmly established and can be changed with exertion and expectation. Here are a few ways to foster a positive cash mentality:

1.   Practice appreciation: Take time every day to ponder the things you are thankful for, including what is going on. Regardless of whether you are battling monetarily, center around the things you do have, like a steady organization of loved ones or a rooftop over your head.

2.   Educate yourself: Read books, pay attention to webcasts, and go to studios or classes on individual accounting and effective money management. The more you know about overseeing cash, the more certain and enabled you will feel.

3.   Set objectives: Put forth sensible monetary objectives for yourself, whether it's taking care of obligation, putting something aside for an up front installment on a house, or putting resources into your retirement. Having explicit objectives at the

top of the priority list can assist you with remaining spurred and centered.

4.   Practice care: Become mindful of your viewpoints and feelings around cash, and work to move pessimistic or restricting convictions to additional good ones. Care practices like contemplation or journaling can be useful in such manner.

5.   Surround yourself with positive impacts: Search out companions, relatives, or coaches who have a positive cash mentality and can uphold you in your endeavors to foster one too. Stay away from pessimistic impacts or individuals who support negative convictions about cash.

All in all, fostering a positive cash mentality is essential for making monetary dependability and progress. By zeroing in on overflow, going ahead with reasonable plans of action, rehearsing appreciation, and being monetarily capable, we can move our attitude from one of shortage and dread to one of overflow and probability.

Chapter 2
Attracting wealth

Drawing in abundance is a point that has acquired ubiquity lately, as an ever increasing number of individuals look to advance their monetary circumstance and accomplish independence from the rat race. While the idea of drawing in abundance might appear as though an otherworldly or elusive plan to some, there are really various down to earth advances that people can take to build their riches and accomplish their monetary objectives. In this article, we will investigate a portion of the procedures that can be utilized to draw in riches and fabricate long haul monetary achievement.

1.   Develop an Abundance Mentality: Perhaps of the main move toward drawing in abundance is fostering an abundance outlook. This includes developing an uplifting outlook towards cash and overflow, and accepting that you are equipped for making monetary progress. Many individuals have restricting convictions around cash that keep them away from

accomplishing their monetary objectives. These convictions might incorporate thoughts, for example, "cash is the foundation of all underhanded" or "rich individuals are ravenous." By testing these convictions and embracing a more sure and plentiful mentality, people can start to draw in abundance into their lives.

2.   Set Clear Monetary Objectives: One more key calculate drawing in abundance is putting forth clear monetary objectives. This includes characterizing precisely exact thing you need to accomplish monetarily, and afterward fostering an arrangement to arrive. For instance, you could define an objective to save a specific measure of cash every month, or to take care of your obligation inside a certain time period. By putting forth clear objectives and making explicit moves to accomplish them, you can begin to draw in abundance into your life.

3.   Practice Appreciation: Appreciation is one more significant figure drawing in abundance. At the point when we center around what we are thankful for in our lives,

we draw in a greater amount of those things into our experience. This is on the grounds that the pattern of good following good expresses that like draws in like - as such, the energy we put out into the universe is reflected back to us. By rehearsing appreciation for the overflow that as of now exists in our lives, we can draw in significantly more overflow and riches.

4.   Take Activity: Drawing in abundance isn't just about certain reasoning and envisioning overflow - it additionally requires making a move. This might include searching out new chances to bring in cash, putting resources into your schooling or abilities, or going into business. By finding a way proactive ways to expand your pay and create your financial stability, you can make a positive criticism circle that draws in much more overflow into your life.

5.   Surround Yourself with Positive Impacts: At long last, it is essential to encircle yourself with positive impacts while trying to draw in riches. This might include searching out guides or good examples who

have made monetary progress, or joining a local area of similar people who are likewise centered around creating their financial wellbeing. By encircling yourself with positive and strong impacts, you can remain roused and enlivened as you make progress toward your monetary objectives.

All in all, drawing in abundance is a diverse cycle that includes fostering an abundance mentality, putting forth clear monetary objectives, rehearsing appreciation, making a move, and encircling yourself with positive impacts. By embracing these systems and earnestly committing to your monetary achievement, you can draw in riches and accomplish long haul independence from the rat race.

Chapter 3
Building financial freedom

Building independence from the rat race is an interaction that includes assuming command over your funds, making a steady groundwork, and growing long haul techniques to accomplish your monetary objectives. Whether you want to resign early, go into business, or basically live serenely without stressing over cash, there are different advances you can take to assemble independence from the rat race.

1.   Create a Spending plan: The most vital phase in building independence from the rat race is to make a financial plan. This includes following your pay and costs and deciding the amount you can stand to spend every month. By making a spending plan and adhering to it, you can abstain from overspending and guarantee that you are setting aside sufficient cash to accomplish your monetary objectives.

2.   Eliminate Obligation: Obligation can be a significant boundary to independence from the rat race, as it can gobble up a huge piece of your pay and keep you from saving and effective money management. Perhaps of the main move toward building independence from the rat race is to wipe out obligation as fast as could be expected. This might include taking care of exorbitant

interest Mastercards, solidifying advances, or revising installment plans with leasers.

3.   Build Crisis Investment funds: One more key consider accomplishing independence from the rat race is developing a crisis investment funds reserve. This ought to be a different record that you add to routinely, and ought to preferably contain sufficient cash to cover 3-6 months of everyday costs. Having a rainy day account can assist you with staying away from monetary pressure and permit you to climate startling costs or employment misfortunes.

4.   Invest for What's in store: as well as killing obligation and building reserve funds, contributing is likewise a significant piece of building independence from the rat race. By putting your cash in stocks, common assets, or different resources, you can develop your riches and make recurring sources of income that can uphold you later on. It is essential to do all necessary investigation and pick speculations that line up with your gamble resilience and monetary objectives.

5.   Create Various Surges of Pay: Building independence from the rat race frequently includes making different floods of pay. This might include beginning a part time job or independent business, putting resources into investment properties, or creating recurring sources of income through ventures or eminences. By enhancing your pay sources, you can decrease your dependence on any one kind of revenue and make more prominent monetary dependability.

6.   Plan as long as possible: At last, building independence from the rat race requires anticipating the long haul. This implies putting forth clear monetary objectives and creating methodologies to accomplish them over the long haul. Whether you want to resign early, purchase a home, or begin a business, it is critical to make a guide that frames the means you will take to accomplish your objectives and the timetable for accomplishing them.

All in all, building independence from the rat race is a cycle that includes making a stable monetary establishment, dispensing with obligation, building crisis reserve funds, contributing for the future, making various floods of pay, and anticipating the long haul. By making these strides and sincerely committing to your monetary achievement, you can accomplish long haul independence from the rat race and make a safer and satisfying life for you as well as your loved ones.

Chapter 4
Managing money

Managing cash is a significant ability that is fundamental for accomplishing monetary steadiness and security. Whether you are attempting to take care of obligation, save for the future, or essentially live inside your means, viable cash the executives is critical to accomplishing your monetary objectives. Here are a few ways to deal with your cash successfully:

1.   Create a Financial plan: Perhaps of the main move toward dealing with your cash is to make a spending plan. This includes

following your pay and costs and putting down a boundary on the amount you can spend every month. By making a spending plan and adhering to it, you can try not to overspend and guarantee that you have sufficient cash to cover your costs and accomplish your monetary objectives.

2.   Prioritize Your Spending: While making a financial plan, it is critical to focus on your spending and spotlight on the costs that are mean quite a bit to you. This might include scaling back optional spending, for example, eating out or purchasing new garments, to let loose cash for additional significant costs like lease, utilities, and reserve funds.

3.   Track Your Costs: One more significant part of dealing with your cash is to follow your costs. This can assist you with recognizing regions where you are overspending and make acclimations to your spending plan depending on the situation. There are many apparatuses accessible to assist you with following your costs, including planning applications and bookkeeping sheets.

4.   Pay Off Obligation: On the off chance that you have obligation, focusing on taking care of it is significant. This might include solidifying exorbitant interest obligation, reevaluating installment plans, or making additional installments to diminish the equilibrium. By taking care of obligation, you can let loose cash for different costs and work on your by and large monetary solidness.

5.   Build a Backup stash: Building a just-in-case account is additionally a significant piece of dealing with your cash. This ought to be a different bank account that you add to routinely, and ought to preferably contain sufficient cash to cover 3-6 months of everyday costs. Having a backup stash can assist you with staying away from monetary pressure and permit you to climate unforeseen costs or employment misfortunes.

6.   Invest for What's to come: as well as building a secret stash, contributing is likewise a significant piece of dealing with your cash. By putting your cash in stocks, common assets, or different resources, you

can develop your riches and make automated sources of income that can uphold you later on. It is essential to investigate as needs be and pick speculations that line up with your gamble resilience and monetary objectives.

7.   Plan for Retirement: At last, dealing with your cash really includes making arrangements for retirement. This might include adding to a 401(k) or other retirement account, as well as fostering an arrangement for how you will deal with your funds during retirement. By anticipating retirement early and routinely evaluating your advancement, you can guarantee that you are on target to accomplish your retirement objectives.

All in all, dealing with your cash actually is fundamental for accomplishing monetary soundness and security. By making a spending plan, focusing on your spending, following your costs, taking care of obligation, fabricating a backup stash, contributing for the future, and anticipating retirement, you can assume command over your funds and accomplish your monetary objectives.

Chapter 5
Overcoming Obstacles

Hindrances are a characteristic piece of life, and everybody faces them all at once or another. Whether it's an individual test, a mishap at work, or a tough spot in your own life, impediments can be disappointing and deterring. Nonetheless, with the right mentality and approach, it is feasible to conquer deterrents and arise more grounded and stronger. Here are a few systems for conquering snags:

1.   Reframe Your Viewpoint: The manner in which you ponder an obstruction can fundamentally affect your capacity to defeat it. Rather than considering a deterrent to be a road obstruction, attempt to rethink it as a test or a potential chance to learn and develop. This can assist you approach what is going on with a more sure mentality and increment your inspiration to track down an answer.

2.   Break the Issue Down: When confronted with a perplexing or overpowering impediment, it very well may be useful to separate it into more modest, more reasonable pieces. This can assist you with zeroing in on each issue in turn and keep you from becoming overpowered. Moreover, separating the issue can assist you with recognizing possible arrangements and foster a game plan.

3.   Seek Help: You don't need to confront impediments alone. Looking for help from companions, family, or an expert can be a compelling method for conquering hindrances. Conversing with somebody about your difficulties can give a new point of view and assist you with rethinking what is going on. Moreover, having somebody to rest on can offer close to home help and assist you with remaining spurred.

4.   Take Activity: While confronting an obstruction, it tends to be not difficult to become deadened by dread or vulnerability. Be that as it may, making a move is much of the time the most effective way to defeat the obstruction and push ahead. Indeed, even

little advances can have an effect, and making a move can assist you with gathering speed and gain certainty.

5.　　Learn from Disappointment: Disappointment is a characteristic piece of defeating obstructions, and it is essential to gain from it. Rather than survey disappointment as an impression of your capacities, consider it to be a valuable chance to learn and get to the next level. Dissect what turned out badly and recognize what you can do another way later on. With every disappointment, you can acquire significant bits of knowledge that can assist you with conquering future hindrances.

6.　　Stay Determined: Conquering snags frequently requires constancy and persistence. It might require investment to track down an answer, and mishaps are probably going to happen en route. In any case, remaining steady and focused on your objective can assist you with beating even the most difficult snags.

All in all, conquering impediments is a significant piece of self-improvement and advancement. By reexamining your viewpoint, separating the issue, looking for help, making a move, gaining from disappointment, and remaining tireless, you can beat deterrents and arise more grounded and stronger. Keep in mind, obstructions are a potential chance to learn and develop, and with the right attitude and approach, you can beat any test that comes your direction.

Chapter 6
<u>Cultivating abundance mentality</u>

Developing an overflow attitude is a mentality shift that can assist you with drawing in additional valuable open doors, joy, and accomplishment into your life. An overflow mindset is a conviction that there are limitless open doors and assets accessible to you, and that achievement and bliss are not restricted to a chosen handful. Here are a few systems for developing an overflow mindset:

1.   Focus on Appreciation: Appreciation is an incredible asset for developing an

overflow mindset. By zeroing in on what you are thankful for in your life, you can move your concentrate away from shortage and towards overflow. Make a propensity for recording a couple of things you are thankful for every day, and consider these things at whatever point you really want an increase in energy

2.   Practice Liberality: When you practice liberality, you are building up the conviction that there is sufficient to go around. This can assist you with developing an overflow attitude by moving your concentrate away from shortage and towards overflow. Liberality can take many structures, for example, giving cash or time to a foundation, proposing to help a companion out of luck, or essentially offering somebody a commendation.

3.   Visualize Achievement: Representation is an integral asset for developing an overflow mindset. Take a period every day to picture yourself prevailing in your objectives and accomplishing your fantasies. This can assist you with zeroing in on the wealth of

chances accessible to you and build up the conviction that achievement is inside your span.

4. Embrace Disappointment: Anxiety toward disappointment can keep us down and keep us from chasing after our objectives. In any case, embracing disappointment as a characteristic piece of the growing experience can assist us with developing an overflow mindset. Whenever we consider inability to be a valuable chance to learn and develop, we are bound to face challenges and seek after our objectives with certainty.

5. Practice Care: Care is the act of being available at the time and noticing our considerations and feelings without judgment. At the point when we practice care, we can turn out to be more mindful of our negative idea examples and convictions about shortage. By noticing these considerations and convictions without judgment, we can start to move our mentality towards overflow.

6.   Surround Yourself with Overflow: Attitude Individuals Encircling yourself with individuals who have an overflow mindset can assist you with developing your own overflow mindset. Search out companions, associates, and tutors who have confidence in the overflow of chances and assets accessible to them. Their positive mentality can assist you with moving your own viewpoint towards overflow.

All in all, developing an overflow mindset is a mentality shift that can assist you with drawing in additional potential open doors, satisfaction, and accomplishment into your life. By zeroing in on appreciation, rehearsing liberality, picturing achievement, embracing disappointment, rehearsing care, and encircling yourself with overflow attitude individuals, you can develop an outlook of overflow and draw in more overflow into your life.

Chapter 7
Leveraging Networks and Relationships

In the present interconnected world, utilizing organizations and connections is significant for individual and expert achievement. Building solid associations with others can assist you with accomplishing your objectives, whether it's getting another line of work, beginning a business, or basically extending your group of friends. Here are a few techniques for utilizing organizations and connections:

1.   Be Veritable and Credible: While building connections, it's vital to be real and genuine. Individuals can tell when somebody is being contemptible or simply attempting to involve them for their own benefit. Center around building genuine, significant associations with others in view of shared trust and regard.

2.   Cultivate a Different Organization: Having an assorted organization of contacts can open up new open doors and points of

view. Try to interface with individuals from various businesses, foundations, and societies. Go to systems administration occasions and join gatherings or associations that line up with your inclinations and objectives.

3.   Offer Worth to Other people: While connecting with others, giving something of significant worth as a trade off is significant. This could be pretty much as straightforward as offering your mastery or guidance, or interfacing somebody with a significant contact. By offering worth to other people, you can construct trust and reinforce your connections.

4.   Maintain Connections: Over the long haul major areas of strength for building takes time and exertion. Try to keep in contact with your contacts consistently, whether it's through email, online entertainment, or in-person gatherings. Commend achievements and triumphs with your contacts, and deal support during testing times.

5.   Use Innovation to Remain Associated: Innovation has made it simpler than any time in recent memory to remain associated with others. Use instruments like LinkedIn, Facebook, and Twitter to remain associated with your contacts and grow your organization. Join online networks and discussions connected with your inclinations and objectives, and participate in discussions with others.

6.   Seek Out Mentorship: Having a coach can be important for expert and self-improvement. Search out people who have made progress in your field or industry, and inquire as to whether they might want to tutor you. Tutors can give direction, exhortation, and backing as you explore your vocation and individual life.

Taking everything into account, utilizing organizations and connections is a fundamental part of individual and expert achievement. By being certifiable and bona fide, developing a different organization, offering worth to other people, keeping up with connections over the long haul, utilizing innovation to remain associated, and searching out mentorship, you can serious areas of strength for construct that will assist you with accomplishing your objectives and grow your chances.

Chapter 8
Investing in yourself

Putting resources into yourself is a strong method for working on your abilities, information, and by and large prosperity. Whether you're hoping to propel your vocation, work on your wellbeing, or just expand your viewpoints, putting resources into yourself can deliver profits in both the short and long haul. Here are a few methodologies for putting resources into yourself:

1.   Education and Expertise Building: One of the best ways of putting resources into yourself is by seeking after instruction and ability building amazing open doors. This could incorporate taking classes or studios to master new abilities, going to gatherings and workshops to extend your

insight, or chasing after postgraduate educations or confirmations to improve your certifications.

2.   Personal Turn of events: Putting resources into your self-improvement can assist you with working on your ability to understand individuals on a deeper level, mindfulness, and by and large prosperity. This could incorporate exercises like reflection, yoga, treatment, or instructing. By dealing with your psychological and close to home wellbeing, you can turn out to be stronger and better prepared to deal with life's difficulties.

3.   Health and Wellbeing: Putting resources into your wellbeing and health can take care of in the long haul by assisting you with keeping up with your physical and psychological well-being. This could incorporate exercises like ordinary activity, smart dieting, getting sufficient rest, and diminishing pressure. By focusing on your wellbeing and wellbeing, you can work on your personal satisfaction and forestall future medical issues.

4.   Networking and Relationship Building: major areas of strength for building with others can open up new open doors and backing your own and proficient development. Put resources into building associations with partners, tutors, and others in your field. Go to systems administration occasions and partake in web-based networks to grow your organization.

5.   Hobbies and Imaginative Pursuits: Putting investment in side interests and innovative pursuits can give a feeling of satisfaction and assist you with growing new abilities. Whether it's playing an instrument, painting, or learning another dialect, taking part in imaginative pursuits can assist you with taking advantage of your innovativeness and fabricate certainty.

6.   Financial Preparation and Effective money management: Putting resources into your monetary future can give genuine serenity and set you up for long haul achievement. This could incorporate exercises like making a financial plan, taking care of obligation, and putting resources

into stocks, land, or different resources. By assuming command over your funds and contributing shrewdly, you can create financial momentum and make a safer future for yourself.

All in all, putting resources into yourself is a strong method for working on your abilities, information, and generally prosperity. By chasing after schooling and expertise building open doors, putting resources into self-improvement and wellbeing, systems administration and building connections, participating in side interests and imaginative pursuits, and making arrangements for your monetary future, you can make a really satisfying and effective life. Keep in mind, putting resources into yourself is a long lasting excursion, so show restraint, remain on track, and partake all the while.

Chapter 9
Creating multiple income streams

Making numerous revenue streams can give monetary soundness and adaptability, as well as the capacity to seek after your interests and interests. By differentiating your pay sources, you can safeguard yourself against monetary difficulties and set out additional open doors for growing long term financial stability. Here are a few systems for making different revenue sources:

1.   Start a Side Business: Beginning a side business can give an extra kind of revenue while likewise permitting you to seek after your interests and interests. This could incorporate selling items or administrations web based, outsourcing, or beginning a counseling business.

2.   Invest in Land: Putting resources into land can turn out both aloof revenue through investment properties and likely long haul appreciation. This could incorporate buying investment properties, flipping houses, or putting resources into land venture trusts (REITs).

3.   Participate in the Sharing Economy: The sharing economy has opened up new

open doors for procuring pay on an adaptable timetable. This could incorporate driving for ride-sharing administrations like Uber or Lyft, leasing an extra room on Airbnb, or leasing your vehicle on Turo.

4.   Invest in Stocks and other Monetary Resources: Putting resources into stocks, securities, common assets, or other monetary resources can give both likely long haul development and automated revenue through profits and interest installments. This requires cautious examination and investigation to distinguish quality ventures.

5.   Create Computerized Items or Administrations: Making computerized items or administrations, for example, digital books, online courses, or programming programs, can furnish a wellspring of recurring, automated revenue with negligible continuous exertion once the item is made.

6.   Rent out Your Resources: Leasing resources you currently own can furnish an extra kind of revenue with insignificant speculation. This could remember leasing a

space for your home, leasing your vehicle or hardware, or leasing extra room.

7.   Participate in Member Showcasing: Subsidiary showcasing includes advancing items or administrations for the benefit of one more organization in return for a commission on any subsequent deals. This should be possible through a site or online entertainment stages.

All in all, making different revenue streams can give monetary soundness, adaptability, and the capacity to seek after your interests and interests. By beginning a side business, putting resources into land and monetary resources, taking part in the sharing economy, making computerized items or administrations, leasing resources, and taking part in member promoting, you can differentiate your pay sources and create financial stability over the long run. Keep in mind, making numerous revenue streams requires cautious preparation and exertion, yet the prizes can be significant.